CALL ME WHEN YOU WANT TO TALK
ABOUT THE TOMBSTONES

Call Me
When You
Want to Talk
About the
Tombstones

Cynthia Marie Hoffman

PERSEA BOOKS
A Karen & Michael Braziller Book

Persea Books, Inc.
277 Broadway
New York, New York 10007

Library of Congress Cataloging-in-Publication Data

Names: Hoffman, Cynthia Marie, author.
Title: Call me when you want to talk about the tombstones : poems / Cynthia Marie
Hoffman.
Description: First edition. | New York : Persea Books, [2018] |
"A Karen & Michael Braziller Book."
Identifiers: LCCN 2017055943 | ISBN 9780892554898 (softcover : acid-free paper)
Classification: LCC PS3608.O47765 A6 2018 | DDC 811/.6--dc23
LC record available at https://lccn.loc.gov/2017055943

Book design and composition by Rita Lascaro
Typeset in Celeste
Manufactured in the United States of America.
Printed on acid-free paper.

Contents

But when the frosts of age settle on our temples,
no spring succeeds, no summer, no autumn.
This cold grave is all we are to look for.
—EPHRAIM PATTERSON SHANNON,
IN A LETTER TO "MY DEAR SON," 1849

What if I croak before it's done?
—DIANE BAKER HOFFMAN, 2008

This Is
Your
Family
Tree

Rose Hill Cemetery, Grave of Kittie Baker Shannon [April, 1936]

This is Mount Carmel, Illinois. In the graveyard, charcoal on my
fingers, rain and silence. The umbrella shrugs its shoulders in
the grass. Seventy years since the earth swallowed this mound of
flowers, we have found this place. The lump still in its throat. It is
October. No birds. We are just beginning to learn the importance
of full names in the history. My mother, Diane Baker Hoffman,
disappears just behind the hill, the length of paper flapping
behind her like a cape. She searches for the others. I am the one
taking a photograph of her.

My mother inherited this leather box that was her grandmother's. She has filled it with things her grandmother collected, things her grandmother's mother collected, and so on. My mother shows me the box, says, I used to take this box with me to camp. We were poor in those days. I didn't even have a suitcase. Just a box with a rope tied around it.

The woman at the City Hall made three photocopies from the Register of Marriages. She stamped the pages in red ink FOR GENEALOGICAL PURPOSES ONLY.

Ephraim Patterson Shannon James Shannon Samuel Shannon Thomas Jenkins Shannon Sarah Jenkins Shannon Thomas Shannon Biddle Thomas Shannon infant Ephraim Patterson Shannon Samuel Shannon Kittie Baker Shannon Mary Frances Shannon Fannie Shannon Baker William Shannon Meriwether Hughes William Shannon Hughes John Samuel Shannon Baker Diane Baker

Down the hill from the graveyard is the best ice cream store in Sunbury, Pennsylvania. It's right down this street. Remember? Turn left here.

There were three Samuel Shannons. Samuel Shannon Samuel Shannon Samuel Shannon.

This leaf has a thousand sisters. All of them, this time of year, blonde. This is a photograph of my mother, standing in the rain on the brick road at Cherry Street, surrounded by the yellow leaves, slick and flat.

How do I write this so it's clear? I can't see the Samuels.

It was an old-fashioned ice cream bar with swivel stools. You remember the swivel stools. Maybe it's on the next street. Head up to the graveyard again. Let's go down the other direction. Try another street over. I swear it was right here. On one of these streets.

One of the Samuels isn't on the tree. Count them. Samuel
Shannon. Samuel Shannon.

I found another paper late last night about Samuel Shannon.
Someone had a miserable typewriter!

Oh yes that was the Herrs Ice Cream. That bakery, you know
they have a factory right next door, they tore it down. Tore all the
houses on the whole block down. All those cute little old houses.

Can you read this?

Here is the list of the reinterred bodies. William was the missing
child. And where is Samuel? Why can't we find him? Where is his
wife? Of course it doesn't list Thomas Jenkins. He's the one who
lived.

And what was happening in the meantime?

In the meantime, Thomas Jenkins went on with his life and
Samuel Shannon went on with his life.

That damn bakery.

The wind blows in through the screen door. The papers flutter
and lift into the air with the curve of a wave but turn away from
the shore, slap down again on the glass table. Nothing ever fully
arrives. No one makes it home.

We weren't able to find out a thing about her, except that her name
was Margaret.

* * * * *

My mother and I walk at Rose Hill. We photograph each other bending toward the names that belong to us: our Kittie, our Most Excellent Samuel Shannon. It is raining.

Though we expected the dead, there is nothing but grass, trees. Only the stones in their various shades of gray to disrupt the gentle arch of the hill as it dips into the valley.

The rain touches everything, indiscriminate, creeps into the ruffled folds even before the carnation touches the stone.

This is a map of the graveyard. I stand above the grave of Kittie Shannon. The tree is a mathematical structure. Some say the roots are a mirror image of the tree itself.

One requires an imagination to visit with the dead in such a place.

Have you ever stopped to think how many drops of blood are in your body that are actually related to these people? Maybe half a drop.

A carnation is nothing. How much does it weigh?

Both graves, in the photographs, the days of their funerals, you can't tell one from the other. Our Kittie our Samuel, buried in pounds and pounds of flowers.

What happens to the coffin when it rains? No one tells you these things.

A raindrop falls. Our image slips along its glassy surface, the living and the dead all of us. Look quick, your stone face, your cold body beneath the umbrella plummeting to the earth.

What do you think they're thinking down there for nearly two hundred years? Are they sick of what they're wearing? And what has become of his cufflinks?

My mother's body in a raindrop, a flash in a crystal ball no bigger than a fingernail, smaller than a fingernail.

Are they not like sunken ships? Can we not think that of them, lying in the dark, blind? But don't tell me. I don't want to know.

I don't want to think about that. I want to be more related than that.

If we have seen the photographs, read the letters in their own handwriting, the ink from their pens. The pen in the hand. If we entered their house.

The graveyard was quite lovely. Don't you think it was lovely, how quiet it was?

* * * * * *

It's all just bits and pieces.

Mary. Mmmm-something Baker. I can't tell what it is. Elizabeth starts-with-an-M Baker.

The middle name of one of the brothers was DeWitt. And you know I have a photograph of a DeWitt. I have to look at it again. Some sort of Civil War costume. It said *my mother's brother* but maybe it didn't say anything. Now I'm thinking it didn't say anything. I just don't know anything at all.

I found a little Sucrets box of glass round things, one of Granddad's little collections of things no else would know what to do with. I also have his teddy bears, and somewhere the little pink sweater Aunt Robin knitted.

Who is this Harriet?

They were from McSomething-or-other Tennessee, four miles southwest of something else I can't read.

Poor Anne Merriweather. Twenty-six children.

I have a well-broken pair of glasses and the leather case he kept them in. And the ring with the set of pearls Samuel Shannon found.

I found two children for Sarah. I gave the three dead infants to Kittie and Samuel Shannon. That was a mistake.

It says Mary Ellen but I know it was Eleanor. She came from France. These were the French people.

This one says *Aunt Fannie*. This one, *my grandfather.* I wish we knew who wrote that.

I just talked to Eleanor Hughes. You know that picture I have in the living room of William Henry Hughes holding a baby? That's who she is! I just talked to that little baby.

He has a mustache. He's someone's brother. Did I read that someplace?

Christy. Chrystie. Christia. What is *Christia*? Christya. Somewhere there's a will and it's spelled out. C-H-R-Y-S-T-I-A. I just don't know where it is right now. I haven't been working on the Bakers lately.

Who writes on a photograph *my grandmother, my father, my grandfather*? This one is the worst: *my grandfather's twin brother.*

She was Eleanor Ragsdale years ago, and I suppose he died and she married this Norton. She answered the phone *This is Eleanor Norton* and I thought, who is that?

I am also washing today, and packing some dresses, baby clothes. They used to dress the little boys in dresses as well.

I'm not sure the nephews were the brothers or the children.

She's 97 years old now. She's in a nursing home. She didn't know what state she was in.

John Hughes, founder of the Kentucky Hughes, was a man of strongly marked character, so forth and so on. Just skip the next seven pages, that doesn't have anything to do with us.

Put him in the trash. We don't know him. Goodbye! We don't know who you are!

Her brother died in 1893, and that's all he wrote.

They really liked naming people Harriet in those days.

* * * * * *

In Vincennes, Indiana, the house where my mother's mother lived is now a parking lot. The houses on either side stand.

My grandmother's father's jewelry store is a flower shop.

Look, are those the same lampposts?

Who is it we're looking for? Let me write it down. Tell me the names.

My mother's hands are always warm. Here, she poses with her rows of filing containers. Newspaper articles starting from the 1800s, letters starting from the 1800s. Labels and files. She is having the mice removed from the basement. Everything is archived, archival. I am the one taking the photograph.

Can you read this handwriting? What is this name?

It broke my heart, my mother says, to see Samuel Shannon's shaky signature, so like Mother's a month or so before she died.

What does this say? I can't help you. I can't see the document through the phone.

I don't know what I'd do if I didn't have you to talk to.

There is a point in the history at which my mother's little round face like a doll begins to appear. I point to the photograph and say as my mother would say, here is the picnic in the forest. This is John Samuel Shannon Baker sitting at the picnic table, and this is his mother Fannie Shannon Baker.

The handwriting is so shaky. I'm sure it was Kittie.

A dentist once extracted teeth in the living room of my great great grandfather's home. The Shannon home. There are still marks, a circle of worn wood, where he bolted down his dentist's chair.

This one on the end is his sister, Aunt Robin. The man in the military uniform, her husband who died. The little boy, her son who died. And next to him, the girl with chubby knees and a halo of blonde curls is my mother, who lived.

The house receives the ivy like a warm blanket. Kittie was your mother's father's mother's mother.

Why should his name in the records surprise us? As if the past were an imaginary thing.

A neighbor photographs the two of us standing between the lampposts. Behind us, a heartsinking open space where the house once stood. I wear my grandmother's butterfly wing necklace. My mother wears her mother's diamond ring.

As if the ink which trailed behind his wrist were itself a small hallucination creeping across the page. What is history but this motion we make with our hand?

At the pub in Vincennes, my mother and I order the tacos. The sour cream arrives in little cold paper tubes. We squeeze it onto the plate, dip the tacos in.

She is the one who wants to walk on the graves. She brings me to Sand Hill, Rose Hill, Odd Fellows, Riverview.

He really did get married. He really lived. He was born.

I need to go over it some more just to make certain.

* * * * * *

Samuel and
Kittie
Really Are
the Main
People

Shannon House, 119 West Third Street. Interior, Upstairs Bedroom [undated]

The mirror in the corner is obliterated by light. We have even lost a part of the glass bookcase, several dark-spined books. Is this the writing desk beneath which Kittie gathered her skirts? The hand that wrote *I am so cold.* The little drawer from which she drew the envelope. Was Samuel alive? I am asking a question about the sound of the shutter in a carpeted room. In any photograph, the viewer's eye is first drawn to the light. Yes. And this is the bed where they slept.

After Kittie and Samuel, people went on with their lives. The house went on with its life, sold then rented then sold again. In the 1950s there was a parrot in a cage in the bay window that would speak to people passing on the sidewalk.

In the photograph, it is 1897. It is December, though you may have guessed. One of the wooden boards on the porch needs fixing. This is the red door. On the right is your great great grandmother.

These are the original light fixtures. This one, which looks like a peachy jellyfish, glass. To the left is the pump for the cistern. What is a cistern?

This is their daughter in the puff sleeve jacket. The head of a white peony rests in her lap.

HELLO
my name is
DR. GERALD BURKETT

Did you get a picture of the doorbell? Patented Dec 31, 1867. The Wabash County Historical Museum paid for the new roof, sealed the front porch which has never been painted. The museum also did the tuck pointing.

The parrot took meals with the family in the dining room, having a place set at the table.

You can buy a pack of greeting cards with a sketch of the Shannon house, and beneath the sketch it says *The Burkett House.*

These are the billows of your great great grandmother's apron and housedress, her pointed shoes, the scuffs on the points of her shoes. Her bright bare hands. This is how the light embraced the trees just beyond the edge of the lawn.

Samuel and Kittie built this house. The brick path leads straight into the sunlight.

They are still alive, the dentist and Lois Ann. They're just like another set of grandparents, aren't they? says my mother, whose parents died. The Burketts, not old enough to be her grandparents, not old enough to be her parents.

Kittie planted these peonies which have replanted themselves for a hundred and thirty-eight years. Their fragrance, right where the sidewalk splits. One path led to the outhouse.

My Dear Daughter, I have spent a lot of money on the house, hope to leave it in good repair so that if you should return to Mount Carmel you will find a good home or you could sell it at a good price.

When their daughter was an old woman, she started to have little strokes. I want to go back to Mount Carmel, she would say.

One winter night the pipes burst and water flowed. Many ceilings were ruined and fell.

In the photograph, a woman stands near the wall of the house in a long white dress. She is almost phosphorescent in the darkness around her, dark ivy spilling over the balcony.

Kittie's funeral was on a Tuesday afternoon. Three years and eight days before my mother was born.

The windows float in a sea of ivy. Mirrored boats cast in dark waters. Only the back of her head is visible, the dark curls gathered at the nape of her neck where the eager froth of her collar rises to greet them.

Am I in Mount Carmel?, she would say.

Everything was lace back then. The little stool draped in lace. The windows gushing with it. The women's blouses puffing, vaporous.

This is a photograph of the Shannon house when there was nothing but a tree and dirt to surround it. Even the streets were dirt. First house on the block.

Who cut down the vines? Were they washed away with bleach? Who watched them shrivel, who tugged them from the house at just the right moment? Was it gently? With a snap of the wrist? How Kittie loved those vines.

When Samuel Shannon died, all the banks and businesses in Mount Carmel shut down. Everything was quiet. Everything was Samuel Shannon.

I am going to put water and toilet in soon. The good Lord has been very gracious and I know you are the best girl on earth. Pappy.

In the winter, the dentist's wife tells us, when there are no leaves on the trees, you can see all the way to the water. If it's a clear day.

* * * * * *

AN ELEGANT AFFAIR

Was the Reception of Mrs Shannon and Mrs. Baker.

An elegant affair and a social triumph was the reception given by Mrs. Samuel Shannon and Mrs. Roy J. Baker at their residence on Third street Friday. Both afternoon and evening their spacious and beautifully decorated parlors were crowded with guests who thoroughly enjoyed the hospitality accorded them.

Refreshments of the daintiest character were served, and the function was of the most pleasant character in every respect, reflecting credit upon the hostesses who did their part so charmingly.

Friday - Feb - 20 - 1903

Those present in the afternoon were
Mrs. S. J. Lauder
" E. F. Eichorn
" F. B. Parkinson
" G. L. Renner
" J. C. Kelchy & Mother
" G. Laubender

A Most Charming Hostess, Mrs. Samuel Shannon
[Newspaper Clippings, ca. 1903, Private Collection]

Social pleasures marked the passage of a delightful evening. The dining room ornamented with potted plants and trailing vines, white carnations, ferns and smilax, streamers of broad green ribbon. Ice cream served in Lily cups. Salted almonds. Apple pie. Whipped cream. Cranberries. Who would ever leave Mount Carmel? The mellow light of wax candles in the candelabra. And for literary salad, heart-shaped leaves.

Kittie's mother's maiden name was Bannon. Kittie's maiden name was Baker, and her married name was Shannon. Kittie's daughter married a Baker (not of relation). So that's how it went Bannon, Baker, Shannon, Shannon, Baker. That's why it's so confusing.

The dinner was all that the greatest elegance would require and the evening was one of the highest pleasure for all. Can you believe that silliness?

Can you hear the rustling of Kittie's wide skirts against the doorway as we pass into the kitchen?

Twenty guests were present at the old fashioned taffy pulling and made the evening one of great hilarity.

My mother climbs the stairs to the cupola, little windowed room that looks out upon the street, the neighbor's house and the neighbor's house, the first floor roof once fenced in like a deck. Who brought the fence down? What year was that?

On their honeymoon, people thought Samuel was Kittie's father. *Samuel Shannon, Most Excellent Grand High Priest of the Royal Arch Masons of Illinois, though young in years, is gray as a badger.*

There is silence, the click of my camera, the release of my breath after the shutter snaps open again as if from a momentary dream.

In white, out back, a woman wrapped in white, the tassels of her shawl hung on a breeze, her long skirt dusted with snow.

A tall man, a white drooping mustache, watch chain glinting across his chest. At their feet, dark holes in the snow.

Inside, there is nothing. I feel nothing standing here in the cool house, no furniture, the loud echo of emptiness chiming against the walls, each step we take in our heavy heels.

Does the house remember? Samuel yelling through his deafness, as if the whole world were deaf. The hours of silence when he must have grown tired from the effort.

The woman in the shawl, the black boots. She isn't looking at the camera. She smiles at something. This is Kittie.

A peanut contest was held, and after tea, which was daintily served, the rest of the evening was devoted to guessing proverbs. What were they doing with the peanuts?

What is the use of our coming here? To walk the winding staircase, impose our foreign hands on the banister.

We stand at the doorway and pose. I am wearing pants. Pants! My mother is wearing pants. What do we know of them, anyway?

The daintiest of refreshments were served. During the social period, dainty refreshments were served by the hostess. Tea, which was daintily served. Everything was dainty in those days. To touch a thing that once a person whom we could never know touched.

When Kittie would have been one hundred and fifty-five years old, my mother calls the florist in Mount Carmel, orders a bouquet to be placed at her grave.

This living room, a room for the living. Through which the ghostly forms of Kittie and our Most Excellent Samuel Shannon pass, memory or no, past the windows, a dark shadow passing through darkness.

Kittie Shannon's daughter married a Baker. Roy John Baker. Kittie's maiden name was also Baker. So it went Baker, Shannon, Shannon, Baker. That's why it's so confusing. I've said this already, haven't I?

This Friday and Saturday at 7:30 pm, join us for a lamplight tour.

* * * * * *

Fire

Burnt District, Golconda, Illinois [1898, 1903, 1930]

The post office burned twice. It burned again. The wood floor.
The wood stove. The wooden frame. A photo of Dixie the dog. The
space that filled the houses dissolved into the rest of space. A white
tent was raised by the river. What can I say from a photograph
after the fire? The ashes are the same as the dirt. As for the
building tops, I can't think of any Baker name that still exists.
A woman in a bonnet just stands there, looking up at the hills.

On the drive to Golconda, a lone dark tree suffers in the naked field, not a leaf to be seen, and from its black arms, smoke rising. Oh that poor tree, my mother says. That must be painful.

Enter the mountains. The deep white fog. Home of my mother's father's father.

Turn right at the crooked sign. Town of white-haired ladies. Whir of wheels turning beneath their chairs.

The rain slams down on Golconda. In the restaurant, the eyes are hard upon us. Smells like cigars in there, the little booths, cheap Wonder Bread sandwiches. Paper plates. Main Street fills with water. Water Street.

Listen to this one: *After his ice cream trousers were ruined, Samuel Shannon's only consolation was religion.*

The Ohio River crouches in the canyon. Just over that hill there. Do you see it? Can't see anything from here.

I called the church. It wasn't the one we wanted.

The colonel can sink deeper and stay drier than any man in the country.

A century ago the fire bell stood here. In the photograph, you can see the three long posts of the tower and the loop at the end of the rope like a noose awaiting a neck.

The bodies were recovered, burned to a crisp.

They don't write things funny like they did in those days.

And here's a list of things he was buying for his store. *Coffee. Spools of lady's twine. More molasses. Meat plates.*

This was across the street from the J.C. Baker CASH STORE. And the clackety-clack of horses. Or maybe it was thunkety-thunk. All the streets were dirt in those days.

This is the shop that was razed for the floodwall. *Razed.*
Not *raised.* OLD LANDMARKS OF GREAT AGE TORN DOWN.
BUILDINGS THAT HAVE SERVED LONG AND VARIOUS PURPOSES
RAZED. To make room for the floodwall.

Startling visit of the grim reaper to a Golconda home.

This was 1940. The flood was 1937. The fire was 1930. The fire had
already happened. Golconda, not yet a ghost town.

Molasses 25 cents, butter 50 cents, 2 ladies collars, 8 spools ladies
twine. 5 pair slippers. Sugar, ribbon, ladies shoes, one washboard.
Coffee. Two flags. One hat. One package of tobacco. Three gallons of
molasses.

I don't think it was meant to be funny. But I love the grim reaper
thing.

* * * * * *

The man who answers the phone is doing research on undertakers. He recognizes the name. He has a picture of the Old Presbyterian Burying Ground. Of course the church burned down.

In the Pope County Historical Society Museum, Fannie's white nightgown puffed out by a bust, balances on its silvery tripod legs.

In the Golconda photos, you will see an empty lot. This is where John Columbus Baker's house used to be before it burned. In the genealogy, you will see a good photo of their house on Columbus Street. Before it was a hotel. Before it burned.

They call him *J.C.* here in town. Dead a hundred years, they still call him that.

I think I might remember Daddy saying something about a mine in the family, but that was not very interesting to a little girl.

Fannie was the postmistress for many years. At the post office that burned. Three times. At least we know that about her. That and the feldspar mine. Nearly drove the Bakers into the ground.

We the heirs of J.C. and Mary Eleanor Baker (our father and mother) hereby divide our interests. The estate consists of brick warehouse, brick post office, dwelling house, and one vacant lot.

At night, the curator cuts off the light, and the nightgown glows. This is the ghost of Fannie Baker, asleep, upright in an empty room. She must have been very tired.

Golconda Herald. J.C. Baker, 1886. Have just opened a Confectionary on Main Street, opposite the Court House, where I keep constantly on hand a general assortment of Candies, Nuts, and Fruits, such as Pie Fruit in bottles or Cans, fine chewing Tobacco, and Cigars.

This is so sad. These pictures. I wish we had better copies of the Silk Stocking House. All in flames.

They also seemed to be selling off the mine. There was a list of picks and things sold for twelve-hundred dollars. Was that a lot of money?

Months after, the museum curator mails Fannie's nightgown to my mother in a brown paper wrap.

For the sake of continual satisfaction among ourselves, it is the agreement.

Anyway. What is pie fruit in a bottle? Do you drink it?

* * * * * *

At Hotel Sleeping in High Posted Bed [1835]

There is no photograph of Samuel Shannon waking up in the middle of the night. With only the light of the flames sizzling upon the curtains, no one could have captured the blur leaping out of bed with fright. What color were the curtains? What was the name of the hotel? The shock resulted in his death, being 84 years old. There was no newspaper at the time. Even the looking glass in its gilded frame that saw, unblinking, the entire thing, quickly forgot.

I found a book. What kind of book? Just a little book, not longer than your fingers. But who wrote it? I don't know who wrote it. But was it published? No, it wasn't published, it's like all the little books I've been finding. But was it typed or handwritten? Of course it wasn't typed. It's pencil.

There should have been an article about the happening. He was an important man. In town on *a little trip of important business*. Our Samuel Shannon. Isn't it dramatic, the way he died? Poor thing.

Was it a candle? It must have been a candle in those days. Even I don't sleep with the lights on, even with the curtains drawn along the bedposts as they would have done in those days. I'm guessing. It might have been the light that woke him. The sound of his own coughing. The crackling? It could have been the crackling.

I just talked to someone else at the Historical Society. She said it was a two-story house with a porch all around. The funeral director said it had been called the Tionesta Townhouse. He built his funeral home right next door.

They didn't keep death records back then. They didn't keep cause of death. Most of the time, people didn't know what they were dying of.

He has postcards of when the church was still standing. Then there was the fire. Then the hat and cap factory.

The story of Samuel Shannon coming to the states has been written so many times on all these little pieces of paper.

The papers only go back to 1866. Now I have to call the newspaper man.

I thought it was the same story all over again. In such and such a year it burned. This burned. That burned. There isn't a church on the east coast that didn't burn down.

The cause of death was chosen from a list of known fatal diseases. It wasn't very long and all of them guesses. Where do you think they came up with things like *Organic Disease of the Heart?*

It begs the question, what was an eighty-four-year-old man doing on a trip of important business?

Thank heavens he wasn't burned.

The funeral director said there once was a hotel in town torn down to build a boarding house. They found evidence that a fire had gutted one of the rooms. I told him that gave me the chills.

So he died alone.

Everything burns down. And that's the end of the story. And then it burned.

* * * * * *

to Jenkins' Mills. The mill was originally built of stone, and in
time of Indian troubles used as a fort, to which place the families
in the neighborhood resorted in times of danger. On one occasion,
when the Indians were approaching, Mrs. Phoebe Jenkins lay very ill, at
Turtle Creek, of typhus fever; a bedstead with curtains was set up
on a riverboat and Mrs. Jenkins was carried to it in blankets, in which
she was taken to Middletown; the boat kept the middle of the river
and the Indians shot arrows through the curtains from the shores. A
tract on Limestone Run, two hundred acres, purchased of David Kenedy,
and the tract in Dry Valley, in warrantee name of James Jenkins, just
west of the Sneagon three hundred and seventy-six acres, of the date
of October 25, 1785. James died suddenly of pleurisy February 5, 1803,
at the age of forty years. James, Sr., had built the brick house now
occupied by William Elliot in Northumberland, and when James, Jr.,
brought his wife there in a carriage from Philadelphia, the servant,
when he opened the door of the carriage, said, "This is the first
house we have seen since we left Philadelphia."

   James Jenkins left children,--Thomas, who died in South
America; Sarah, married to Ephraim Shannon, whose daughter married
Colonel Alfred Kneass, and is deceased, and her only daughter married
to A. C. Van Alen, of Northumberland, and she died August 2, 1882,
who left a son, Alfred Jenkins Van Alen, who died on August 23,
1882; Elizabeth, married Thomas P. Bonham, and died in Illinois;
Mary, died September 26, 1881, at the age of ninety years; and Miss
Harriet still lives at Northumberland (1886), at the age of eighty-
seven years, in the possession of all her faculties and unimpaired
memory. The mill was rebuilt by Colonel Kneass in 1853-54; again
remodeled to a roller-mill in 1882-83; and again remodeled by A. C.

Phoebe Jenkins with Family, Turtle Creek, Pennsylvania [ca. 1780]

As I lay in my bed, birds pressed their wide black beaks through
the curtains. Some of them flew past so quick they were nothing
but a thin line. I dreamed the bedroom filled with water and the
sound of water. It was as if the whole house rose from the ground.
But it could have been the fever. I reach for my face. When I die, I
will leave this bed to William. Just at this moment, I hear his voice.

Isn't it fun to look in close at the crowd and see all those funny hats? Some are two feet high, I swear it. What are all those wide ribbons spiking up to high heaven? Looks like a fern on a dinner plate.

The brick building is definitely the Beauchamp Chapel, the whole congregation gathered in the sunlight. This was the location of the church in 1877 when the cyclone hit Mount Carmel. Then the clapboard building, I don't know what that is.

Fortunately, she drew an arrow to her head. The woman to her right could not be still. She has no face.

You know about Phoebe, don't you? She was your great great great great grandmother's grandmother. She had some horrible fever. Not Typhoid, I forget, but something horrible. The family carried the whole bed onto the riverboat and rode out to the middle of the river with her on it.

THE CYCLONE! Mount Carmel Devastated! Thirteen Men Killed Outright! Seventy-Five Wounded! A Fire Adds To The Horror Of The Scene! One Hundred Buildings Destroyed! Loss a Half Million Of Dollars! Recovery Of The Bodies! Many Miraculous Escapes!

Reverend Beauchamp was your great great great great great great grandfather. Died on the road, never made it back to Mount Carmel. Your great great great great great great grandmother married him after her first husband was lost at sea.

In times of Indian troubles, the Indians shot arrows through the bed curtains from the shores.

Who takes a photo that's half dirt? The bottom half is dirt. Then there's the crowd, and then there's only up to the stained glass windows. There's more dirt than God.

How old was Phoebe when they carried her to the river? Was she a child?

The air was filled with flying roofs, windows, doors, lumber, rails, clothing, etc. The grand steeple of the Old Methodist Episcopal took wing like an arrow. Its destruction embraced all of Fourth Street. Here is the painting of the Reverend holding his red-spined Holy Bible.

The courthouse is an utter wreck and the jail is nearly so. The following houses are utterly destroyed:

Of course she wasn't a child. She was a grown woman. An old woman. I can see her in my head.

Mrs. Beauchamp's first husband's sister's husband was shot by one of the men aboard his ship. His uncle was lost at sea. His cousin, killed while cutting in a whale.

Frances drew an arrow to her head, thank heavens, for I never would have found her.

Many others will undoubtedly die within a day or two. John Tennis, will probably die soon. Charles Burton and wife, the latter will probably die. Charles Poole, supposed to be buried in the courthouse ruins. Mrs. Aynter was blown into a tree.

At first the church survived. And then it burned.

* * * * * *

I Only Know
What Is
In the
Pictures and
In the
Pictures
No One
Is Moving.
Everyone
Is Still.

Portrait of Thomas Jenkins Shannon with Seated Man (T.J.'s Father?),
[ca. 1840s (?)]

Don't you think they have the same lips? It's hard to tell. Thomas
is the one in the long coat. Seems to need the cane. Wouldn't you
say the man in the chair looks like Abe Lincoln? But nicer. Nicer-
looking. A surf of dark hair. The thing to find out is whether it was
possible to put an image onto paper. This flimsy piece of paper. If
it is not an ambrotype. If it is not a daguerreotype. Whether the
light in his curls is the sunlight or something else.

I am excited that the photo of Thomas Jenkins Shannon with the man in the chair is his father. This is Ephraim. Has to be. Love, Mom.

All of the diaries and photos and scrapbooks and records belong to you. I was the executor of the will and I determined that you should have them.

She who works on it, gets it. That's what I remember her saying.

When we knew he was Ephraim, when I knew, I felt his face appear before me as if for the first time, suddenly a known assembly of features, in my house, in my hands. A photograph I had looked at a hundred times before.

Here is the only photograph of Laura F. Beall, probably a year old, a bow on her shoulder, dimples at her knuckles. I don't know what the *F* is for. Here is her mother, Mabel.

And I had thought, here he is. He sits in the chair. His hands are folded in his lap as if in prayer, in meditation: *I am Ephraim. I am Ephraim. I am Ephraim.*

Laura Beall had a cat who wrote letters to her cousin's cat. Her name was Laura. They sure liked naming people Laura in those days. The women, not the cats.

Dear Diamond, Love Sweetie. How would a letter like that go? There was no will. Who came for the cat?

Dear Marce and Shannon. At long last I have finally put down all the dates I can think of. I am also enclosing some old family pictures you may find interesting. The ones I want returned I have marked with a small "x" on the back.

I know who she is. The last living heir to the old-growth forest. The White Oak is the state tree of Illinois. The Tulip Tree. Laura Forest Beall.

Dear Diamond, I am not sure what more I am to do but wait. I slept on her belly but something was amiss. The cabinets are shut tight. I am hungry, Diamond, and the dust just sits in the air. My breath alone is not enough to stir it. Sweetie.

I had said, there's no picture of him, we have no picture of him. I wish we knew what he looked like. I had stood above his grave, though at my feet only the grass was visible. And now, look at his wavy hair!

The roots of the tree are only two feet deep. But they spread out really far.

I am certainly a poor kitty now, my dearest Diamond. The loggers have come to take the forest, I know it. The floorboards rumble in a way that never my purring could bring about.

In any other album, in the great diaspora of unknowable papers, the man in the chair would be only a man, like any other man, big hands, dark eyes fixed just outside the camera's lens so as to not ever quite meet your eyes. Ephraim, I say, but he does not answer.

All the roots in the forest spread out and become entangled in each other, as if they were holding hands.

If your Laura should come to visit, tell her Sweetie crept out the back door.

* * * * * *

Portrait of Thomas Jenkins Shannon with Seated Man (~~T.J.'s Father?~~),
[ca. ~~1840s (?)~~ 1870s]

Though Thomas, standing, rests his hand upon the seated
man's shoulder, the Man in the Chair cannot be his father. The
photograph was torn from its cardboard host, and this is why.
Because of their wide lapels, their voluminous sleeves. Fawn
trousers are a dead giveaway. Note the north light. Note *albumen.*
The ghost that came into my room has gone again. What if I
called him Ephraim, and that was not his name. You must resign
yourself. The possibility does not exist. Even on a clear day.

Dear Diane. Don't you think it is time for us to dispense with the formal "Mrs."? I have found someone to clean Jesse G.'s gravestone and then we will have a photograph taken of the stone without its moss.

This is the best photographic paper available in color. It's rated at 75 years, guaranteed.

Why didn't I take a photograph of the Beall Woods sign? We could have gotten out of the car on our way to Mount Carmel. Laura Forest's tombstone was the tallest in the graveyard, white as a birch.

I told her you didn't have to pay her one bit, but I said Diane will probably disagree.

You've seen this photograph before. Roy John Baker and Samuel Shannon sitting together on the trunk of a fallen tree. Look, I never noticed his eyes are closed. Roy John's eyes are closed. He's smiling. Samuel Shannon holds the cane.

This is Annie Hughes with the famed American dentist of Calcutta. Looks like German traditional dress. See the photograph is printed *Köpenhamn*. She had returned to Mount Carmel for her mother's death, but the dentist had not.

Less than a human lifespan, and that's if we're lucky.

We were hungry. We weren't in the mood for photographs. You remember we got to the courthouse, we sat in the car eating crackers. Anyway, it is always possible to go back to Mount Carmel.

We walk around the house with blinders on, reaching into the dark files, boxes deep as a grave.

You have to forget I told you that photo on the fallen tree was Roy John Baker with Samuel Shannon. It's not. Roy John's eyes are closed, that's true. But the man beside him is John Columbus Baker.

Is that snow in the photograph, or is it old?

And you remember his daughter. The nightgown hanging in Golconda. Here, put it on. Take your hair down. Try to look like she looked. Put your hands in your lap. Put your hand on the arm of the chair. Why do you have your shoes on?

Once you start to memorize the photographs, the long white beard is unmistakable. This newspaper article, clipped with a rushed hand. This photograph brittle as a crumb.

Of course it's been washed. What does it smell like? Any specks of dust, a Fannie speck, long since washed away. This gown is a tent, up to my neck, down to my ankles.

This is the one photo we have of Annie, in that silly hat.

Do you think she would have had her photograph taken in her nightgown? Isn't it indecent?

Here is a postcard of the house. Someone has written *Here I was born*.

* * * * * *

*The Man in the Chair, Shown with Victorian Sitting Chair, Sitting
[ca. ~~1840s (?)~~ 1870s]*

He lived. He had a life. What was it?

I Love
You
Mary Wilson

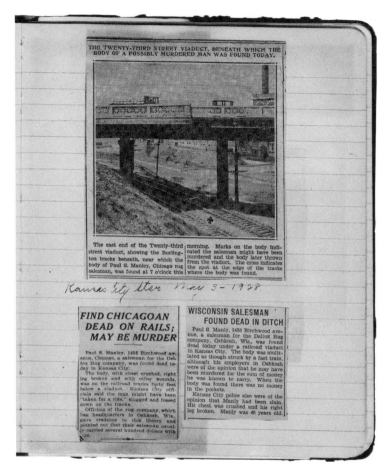

THE TWENTY-THIRD STREET VIADUCT, BENEATH WHICH THE BODY OF A POSSIBLY MURDERED MAN WAS FOUND TODAY.

The east end of the Twenty-third street viaduct, showing the Burlington tracks beneath, near which the body of Paul S. Manley, Chicago rug salesman, was found at 7 o'clock this morning. Marks on the body indicated the salesman might have been murdered and the body later thrown from the viaduct. The cross indicates the spot at the edge of the tracks where the body was found.

Kansas City Star May 3 - 1928.

FIND CHICAGOAN DEAD ON RAILS; MAY BE MURDER

Paul S. Manley, 1456 Birchwood avenue, Chicago, a salesman for the Dellox Rug company, was found dead today in Kansas City.

The body, with chest crushed, right leg broken and with other wounds, was on the railroad tracks forty feet below a viaduct. Kansas City officials said the man might have been "taken for a ride," slugged and tossed down on the tracks.

Officials of the rug company, which has headquarters in Oshkosh, Wis., gave credence to this theory and pointed out that their salesman usually carried several hundred dollars with him.

WISCONSIN SALESMAN FOUND DEAD IN DITCH

Paul S. Manly, 1456 Birchwood avenue, a salesman for the Dellox Rug company, Oshkosh, Wis., was found dead today under a railroad viaduct in Kansas City. The body was mutilated as though struck by a fast train, although his employers in Oshkosh were of the opinion that he may have been murdered for the sum of money he was known to carry. When the body was found there was no money in the pockets.

Kansas City police also were of the opinion that Manly had been slain. His chest was crushed and his right leg broken. Manly was 45 years old.

Dead on Rails; May be Murder [Newspaper Clipping, Kansas City Star, May 3, 1928. Scrapbook, Private Collection]

The X indicates the spot at the edge of the tracks where the body was found. The theory police formed from the three pools of blood was that the fall from the viaduct did not bring instant death, but that he struggled to three different spots before death came. He died with a telegram in his pocket congratulating him on the amount of business he had done. He had sold a great many rugs before he died.

Her husband's chest was *crushed.* Or Mary Wilson's chest was crushed. *Body mutilated as though struck by a fast train.* This is exactly what it says.

Mary Wilson didn't cut straight. Mary Wilson didn't organize this book very well. I wish she had written on this page. Who is this article about? Why are all these poems in here? I don't know what this is.

This is the woman who keeps escaping my book.

No one cut straight in those days. Look at these newspapers! You can hardly read this. *The body was still limp when found.*

Hallowe'en Greeting take it from me, on Hallowe'en night, don't go out alone or you'll get a fright love Henrietta. Ship Body Home. Unique Recipe and Jelly Shower for the Bride-Elect.

I put a lot of photos in the books. There were so many loose photos. They are better in the books, even out of order. They were out of order to start off with, so it shouldn't make a difference. But where is Mary Wilson?

Former Pastors of Church Send Hearty Greetings. Dr. Miles' Nervine has been wonderfully successful in revitalizing the nerves of thousands of delicate women.

Can we blame her for her crooked pasting? Think of the glue sticky on her fingers. How she touched her eyes, how they stung. Of course this is all conjecture.

Now where has Mary Wilson gone? How could she have fallen out again? Why can't I keep track of her?

Young Couple Happily Mated. A Silver Shower. A Beautiful Wedding. Consumption Claims Victim. Colorado Team Makes Fifty-Seven Points Against Denver.

I found Mary A. Wilson. It's terrible. She has the biggest nose you ever did see. And is that a hat on top of her head or is that her hair?

He was dressed in a light gray suit. No hat was found near the scene. In the evening, white crumbles of glue tumbling to her skirts as if the little stars were rolling out of the sky.

I love you Mary Wilson. Your memory, which I can't remember. Everything you saved.

The Dozen Club Enjoyed Breakfast in the Woods, Prepared and Ate Breakfast Gypsy Fashion. Sudden Termination of Life. Rug Salesman Dies Beneath Viaduct: Accidental Plunge and Suicide Theories Also Being Considered.

Mary Wilson is home! While walking this morning, I remembered I'd put her in my mother's album that only has the little gift cards. I love that book.

Anthropometric Laboratory 1933. Age 45. 2 brothers. 5 sisters. Widowed. Hair color dark brown. Eye color blue. Iris clear. Eyebrows concurrency small. Eye obliquity small.

Mary A. Wilson was not Mary Wilson. Mary Wilson was the one with the flawless skin. *Occidental flattening absent. Facial asymmetry absent.*

I love you, Mary Wilson. Mary Wilson, whoever you were.

Bizygomatic. Bigonial. Tragion. Acromion. Dactylion. Biacromial. Earlobe free. Body build medium. Handedness right. Small overbite. Small freckles.

* * * * * *

Corpse
Under Local
Excess

Shannon House, Rear View, Samuel Shannon, Standing [undated]

A brief synopsis of the known world: a plot of space marked by a fence. Particles of white shuttled through the air. A man comprised of flesh, a white beard. No shadow pinned to his boots. Regarding the second man, the evidence points to snow. Do the records say what type of business he ran? How he gestured? Whether he was rowdy or quiet in the evenings? *I'm so darned deaf tonight, I couldn't hear a mill whistle.* That was something he used to say. *I know when I say good bye to Pappy this time I will never see him alive again.* Something his daughter said.

Our Most Excellent Samuel Shannon Grand High Priest of the State of Illinois sits on the porch with his wife, who appears to be knitting, or her hands appear to be poised in midair above her lap. A dark room of ivy they sit in.

Samuel Shannon. Oh gosh, he had a mill and he was also a banker. He also had a shop. He sold goods. And he also had a church. Basic things like shovels, nails. Methodist it was.

Mr. Shannon was knocked down and rolled under the mud guard of the machine, the wheels fortunately not striking him. During the excitement following the arrival of Mr. Shannon at his home, Mrs. Shannon was also injured when she slipped on a rug and fell.

Whoever takes the photograph calls out from the lawn. Ivy and ivy and ivy.

Uncle Sam threatened with pneumonia. Better come at once. Answer.

The granary is gone now. Go down where the plumbing place is, you'll see a big bluff and the IGF Grocery store. On the right is where it was, on Walnut Street.

Samuel Shannon Narrowly Escapes Death Saturday Evening. Was Avoiding Speeding Auto When He Stepped in Front of Slow One.

The thing about snow is that it was an occasion. Even in Illinois. That's why you see the Most Excellent Samuel Shannon tobogganing, rolling a snowman, his bright moustache like a smear of snow across his lip.

Roy John Baker: Mr. Shannon much better, no fever.

In this photograph, mostly darkness. The only indisputably visible thing: Samuel's crisp white sleeves. Is he looking at the camera? Who can see a thing with all that ivy?

Sam Shannon boarded a toboggan about 10:30am Friday and hasn't been heard from since.

Cherry Street is the house with the red brick. Cherry is the Beall house.

Wilcox Wholesale Grocery Outlet is 9th Street between Walnut and Chestnut, the red brick road. It is now the Sharp & Williams Plumbing Company. Stop the car. I'll take the picture through the window.

Roy John Baker; Home at six your father sitting up. Mother. 10:03am

Samuel Shannon Barely Misses Serious Injury. Mr. Shannon did not hear the car backing toward him, and it struck him in the back, knocking him down. This is Mr. Shannon's second encounter with an automobile in the past year.

Know ye, our Most Excellent Companion Samuel Shannon reclines fully dressed on a beach towel. The surf whispers, Alhambra. California. Miles from home. Here he is with his hat. Here he is without his hat. Guess in which photograph he was sick.

* * * * * *

Shannon House, Front View, Kittie Baker Shannon [1924]

Eighty four years since, the exterior renovations are now complete.
The red door is now green. The porch now painted that has always
been bare. When Kittie pushed the lawnmower through this
yard in her long skirts, hot as blazes. While in Alhambra, on the
opposite coast, the breeze had just set in from the ocean. She like
a tall leaf clinging to the brick of this empty house. Do you think
she regretted staying home? If she would have known what would
happen. Whose house is this? Now the ivy is gone. Where is the
peach tree? Samuel's corpse was carried home by train.

He had been in California for several weeks, having gone for a visit with his daughter.

I am trying to show Pappy as much pleasure as I can for it is the only time I have ever had to do anything for him farther than buy him a pair of socks.

My Dear Husband, it seems like a hundred years since you left.

Pappy says he has been too cold ever since he has been here. I give him at lunch and again at night the top glass off a quart of milk.

So far as I am concerned I do not care whether I ever see Mount Carmel again I know I have not long to live and it makes little difference where I die I only came here because I wanted to see the children once more and I know it was my only and last chance. Do not tell Fannie what I say or do not write anything you do not want her to hear she always reads your letters.

Little Shannon is having a fine time flying his kite the last few days he sure has more fun than Robin. Life is the real thing to her.

Pappy and I were talking the other night how nice it would be to have a house together so you folks could have your own bedroom and an extra room for sewing and us all to be together then we surely could live and die together.

Robin made a lovely apple pie she is some smart kiddie I am telling you.

I got busy and doctored him best I could with an iron tonic. I was trying to rub him and I said, well now if Mother was here she would do this right he said yes she can rub knows how.

On one drive we bought a box of oranges for 25c I counted them 200 oranges what do you think of that.

Mrs. Sam Shannon Papa still sick doctor says not serious but I want you to leave for Los Angeles on train number twenty-five bring Masonic book out of small grip am wiring money.

65

He says as you know little, but the other night he said, your mother needs me. Mother, I need you as well as you both need each other, but what is the use to wait until I am dead or about so before you will be willing to leave that home.

I do not want you to misunderstand me I know you love as Pappy says every brick of that house just ought to be willing to leave it long enough when we all want you so much.

Please inform Mrs. Baker and Mrs. Samuel Shannon escorts of body on your train under local excess 2760007 that I have arranged transfer of body from 3rd St. to Ferry Station.

You know no one is ever sure he never asks for anything just roams around and when we ask him he says, the paper, or, sugar salt, or anything, you know him.

General Baggage Agent. Corpse on local Daylight today to be rechecked to Mount Carmel. Please handle transfer between stations.

I was going to send you a telegram but I was afraid it might frighten you, and that would not be birthday greetings, would it?

He lived long enough to recognize his wife upon her arrival and the end came peacefully a short time later.

I do wish he had been like you Mother dear tried to keep young but he was the kind adversity broke and now he is just a dear sweet old man and I want to make you both happy.

In accord with practicality a unanimous request and desire, all places of business are asked to suspend activities during the hour of the service. It is expected that this will be an unusually large funeral.

Still I think he is homesick when he opened your letter this A.M. he looked up so kind of pathetic and said, she says it seems a hundred years since I went away.

It actually rained here today. Robin and I felt like going out and standing in it.

The Addition
of the
Evil Brother

*Portrait of James Wilcox at Ten Years Old, with Fur Rug and Twisted
Iron Toddler Chair [ca. 1912]*

No one looked directly at the photographer in those days. So that
explains some of it. One would have to be very still. Eyes pale as
glass. Arms dutifully in their place. Does he look like a child who's
been hit by a car? I can't stop staring at his severe widow's peak.
But that was just the way his hair was combed. Does he look the
same, or never the same after? His twin is the one who slept with
a knife under her pillow. He would have been encouraged not to
smile. Just a little something in the lips. You tell me. Her name
was Adah.

I love the addition of the evil brother and why he was so evil, and the strong sister. Makes them seem like real people.

Adah and Jimmie Wilcox were twins. Their parents were Othello Wilcox, you know he had that grocery store in Mount Carmel, that brick building that used to be his store, and their mother was Eleanor Hughes, and she married Othello Wilcox, and so there was Adah and Jimmie. Adah, I think her name was Adah Louise, that's what everybody called her because that was her name. Adah and Jimmie were twins.

Mr. Othello Wilcox, the popular young grocer, received the handsomest Christmas present this morning that has yet come to town. It is a pretty little set of twins.

Jimmie, when he was young, was riding bikes with a friend. It was in the newspaper. He fell with his bike and hit his head on the curb and he was never the same after that. They moved to another state. It seems like Indiana or someplace, but don't quote me. I have to look that up. Don't quote me. I think they moved.

Here is the obituary. *Boy is Laid to Rest. Body Expected to Arrive on Tonight's Train. His unusually sunny disposition endeared him to his hosts of friends.*

Adah was a principal and a physical education teacher, so even as a child she was very strong. Something happened out on the boat. Adah was stronger than Jimmie thought, and he went over, and he didn't come up.

It's funny to think there were curbs in those days. I thought all the streets were just dirt.

Here is the article about Jimmie. Where it says there was a lake accident. I can hardly read this. The first word I can read is *banishments*, no, *blandishments*, what is *blandishments? Not withstanding the heavy traffic prevailing at the time, the two boys chose to go coasting on a bicycle down the Market Street Hill.*

The twins rode together in a wicker stroller shaped like a sleigh. Four giant, airy wheels. A frilly canopy with a pointed top like a circus tent. Both the boy and the girl in bonnets and dresses.

That was when they were children.

Young Smith was riding the wheel, they called bicycles *wheels* in those days, something about *leading to the reunion grounds,* whatever that was, *Wilcox was on the handlebars* something.

The car was hidden from the boys by a wagon and when it turned something *they were going at great speed and were unable to* something *to stop and as a result coasting full-tilt into the side of the automobile.*

Here it says *head-on. Found both boys hanging onto the car.*

Oh, where is the curb.

After the bicycle fall, his father never did anything to discipline him because Jimmie was the son and he was going to take over the business. He was the boy. When they moved, there was a lake. The twins were out on a lake and they were out in the boat. She couldn't take it anymore. Adah was afraid of him.

Young Wilcox was unconscious and was first thought to be dead.

I don't know what he did. What did he do? *His unusually sunny disposition endeared him.*

That was Adah's way of *taking care of him* because he was so mean. That's the way the story went. His father preceded him to the grave.

He was carried to the yard and efforts were made to revive him. Dr. P.G. Manley was summoned something *partially successful efforts to revive him* something something *was badly bruised on the head and concussion of the brain was feared.*

The Smith boy was painfully where is the rest of the article?

It doesn't say anything about a lake accident. Are you sure? His hosts of friends?

When I copied it, it just broke in half I guess.

* * * * *

Ere I
Discerned
It

Samuel Shannon on Deathbed [Letter from J.T. Davis, Boarding House, 1 O'clock Tuesday, March 25, 1845]

Here the consumptive is raised to taste the soup which he does not taste. Nor the lemonade, nor acid water. The flooded pockets of his lungs. The letter says or does not say. Like berries, sour and full, drowned in the juice of their own vigorous making. His name called to no answer. Certainly the fixed gaze. Peeling open the envelope to postscript the sad intelligence of his passing. The meticulous enclosing of his things into a carpet bag. Samuel. Samuel. Samuel. This is how it happened. The poor fellow.

I saw a dead person. I entered the funeral home.

Why can't we find our young Samuel Shannon? Either his body is buried in Florida or his body is buried in Georgia. Either he died in St. Mary's or he died in Glen St. Mary's. Either he died in a hospital or he died as a boarder in a boarding home in St. Mary's or Glen St. Mary's. It was the Syrian Consumption. What is the Syrian Consumption?

When we were lost, I went into the funeral home to see if they could help me. The heavy door, empty house, big house, dark. An open book, an empty page.

Should I call into the room? Dark carpet, dark wallpaper thick as fabric. A stairwell. Winding, of course. A drinking fountain with its silver body clinging to the wall.

If you could have seen him die, smoothe his pillow and wipe as I did the death dew from his brow, and found him always so patient and resigned, it would assured you as it did me, that his last days were his best days.

The row of empty folding chairs, arranged, awaiting the warmth of mourners shifting upon them.

By the side of a spreading live oak tree oh it's an oak tree I thought it was a willow *by an old friend I found lying here* it's just so poetic *sleeps your son and husband. And often as we visit the green graveyard of St. Mary's with the weeping willow* oh now they've changed it to a willow again *and shady grove and quiet resting place we will think of your loss and he will not be forgotten.*

Then I saw the open casket, the ivory silk, the bright hands folded, afloat in the dark puddle of his suit. A head of curls, dull as a wig.

Either it was a willow tree or an oak tree, the tree he was buried under.

How should I tell you if the tree still stands? If his body nourished the tree. If the branch, as an animal stretches its long neck over the edge of a lake, sipped and exhaled.

If it's an oak tree, we're more hopeful.

The Dr. had just arrived when I saw a change (that change which him who have the dying alone can understand) come over him.

If I breathe what the wind has strewn about since the old days. If nothing ever disappears.

Well, a dead person shouldn't bother you. We've been visiting gravesites all day.

But I wasn't looking at any bodies.

If you are sensitive, you may feel yourself rising out of your body. You may feel that others who have risen from their bodies are close to you, even now, as you tend the garden, run the comb through your hair, sit with a book in your lap.

Which graveyard is *the sweetest little graveyard of the South?* It doesn't say that on the list.

If you are sensitive, something hazy may appear in the periphery. Whether it is your great great grandfather's brother, no one has been able to determine.

He fixed his eyes upon me, ere I discerned it his spirit fled forever.

Who leaves the front door unlocked with a body lying there? And who can sleep in a house with the body of a stranger on the first floor? Does the spirit pass up through the floor, through the mattress? Through their bodies as they sleep?

Whether it has a beard, no one can say. Whether it has arms and legs. If it wears a coat.

Sometimes I am not afraid. I want to wake up and Samuel is standing at the foot of my bed. I want to wake up and his breath is on my ear. I want to wake up to a chorus of Samuels.

And how does the spirit escape? Does it snake out the nose? Spill from the ears? Rise from the body prostrate and hover for a moment a body on top of a body as lovers before it scatters into the bodiless world?

Why don't you tell me how to find you? Closed tight in your little wooden room. Are you cold? Have you forgotten your body? Go ahead and come into my room, young Samuel, Consumptive Samuel. Lean toward the light at the curtains. Let me see your face.

To his mother, wife, and other children, to his father and Aunt Harriet of whom he often speaks, to all his relatives, let this letter carry the last expression of affection from the trembling life of your friend.

Or is that the end of it? The lights just go out.

The ghosts of the people we know come, but none of the ghosts of the people we don't.

Here is the list of people buried in St. Mary's Oak Grove Cemetery. Samuel Shannon could be any of these: *Unmarked Slab. Unmarked Slab. Unmarked Slab. Unmarked Slab.*

* * * * * *

I Ain't
Ephraim

Inventory, E.P. Shannon deceased. [Filed October, 1851]

One rocking chair. One pair dining tables (cherry). One cherry rocking chair. Parlor carpet. Sugar tongs. Mantel glass with gilt frame. Lots of sundries in the upper cellar. Lots of books in the bookcase. One dressing glass in the east room upstairs. One looking glass. Dining table, breakfast table, small table, work table. Two old coffee kettles. Yellow Windsor chairs. Walnut bureau. Walnut cupboard. One wagon. Two sleighs. A rockaway. Cradle in the dining room. Crib in the west room. Washstand, basin, pitcher.

My Dear Son, three weeks before your Mother's death, I came into the room one evening. She was all alone and at prayer, there was something peculiarly solemn in her manner and looks. Something indiscernibly heavenly, there seemed to be a holy influence pervading the room.

No one has ever come to claim one of these graves. No, no one knows where the bodies are. They didn't bring the bodies. They left the bodies behind.

How many Ephraims are on the tree? Half of them *aim*, half of them *iam*. You can remember to spell his name with this nifty pneumonic device: *I am Ephr-i-am.*

After I had been in a short time, she said to me, Ephraim, O do help me to intercede for our dear Son, he is going to leave us, he is going to leave his church.

This is the tombstone of Ephraim Patterson Shannon. No, there is no photograph. Here is the stone of his wife, Sarah. No, their bodies are not buried here. Only the tombstones are here.

And I said to her in an assumed careful manner don't fret about Tom, he is not going out of the world. Don't be consumed, he has too much mind for that, but what if he does, he may join the Mormons for what I care.

Except that it's *Ephraim*. Not *Ephriam*. I ain't *Ephraim*.

The stove room seems to suit me best this winter for every time I go out and get damp feet I take a cold that confines me to the house. I am now an invalid, have not left the house for five days past I have taken medicine, bathed feet. Still some headache and pains in my bones.

Of course, they spelled *Shannon* with an *a*. Right on the tombstones. *Shannan*. Those poor little babies. Hardly had a life, and they can't even get the names right on their graves.

The weather for some days past has been mild. The ice gone from the west branch. Blue birds twittering. Snow all melted but it is hailing raining and snowing all together just now we had a pretty cold January about three weeks excellent sleighing.

And little William. Where is he? He was an infant. They may not have left a stone. And James and the two more Ephraims, if someone wants to find them, they're never going to be able to read them. The slate ones, the ones for the boys, are already chipping away.

I have your desk and bookcase placed in the southeast corner of the room it holds all my office books and papers. I have three shelves in the bookcase and filled them with the best books. I have been trying to sell olde Bonny.

The sunken trench of each letter worn into the stone as if a mourner, an army of mourners, had paced in this pattern a hundred and fifty-seven years. *Ephraim Patterson Shannon. Ephraim Patterson Shannon. Ephraim Patterson Shannon.*

Four children dead in nine years. Then a twelve-year respite and another dead. Sarah and Ephraim born three years apart, died three years apart.

We see the hills and valleys covered with snow looking hoary with age. We look with confidence for spring to succeed with all its gay accompaniments, to be followed by the full glows of ardent summer.

As if touching the letters themselves were touching the face of the man. But even his wife was not alive to stand here as I do now. Beneath my feet, nothing. Nothing but a field like any other.

The remaining paper must not be sent blank. Permit an old man to advise you from sad experience, avoid the rocks on which I split. Farewell.

The first hand that touched this stone bore the chisel. And then the hands that carried the stone but left the body behind. And then my hands. And my mother's.

Look at the math. Three children survived.

* * * * * *

Genealogying

Marcel, Shan

St. Jude Hospital Coronary Artery Sketch, Marcella Baker
[Private Collection, ca. 1993]

This is not the x-ray of Shannon Baker's tubercular lungs. The little
white cloud of the 1930s. That ended up in the trash. It is not a
genuine photograph of my grandmother's heart. How she laughed
and laughed in the evenings when she was tired. Not drawn by
the hand of an artist, not even the hand of the only man who
touched her heart, the dark actual lobbing thing. She carried it in
her needlework bag and showed it to everyone. Anything that ever
went into the trash was a mistake. This was her seashell compact,
loose powder. Her mirror. My mother holds it up and says, *do you
see her in there?*

At least we have the monkey he carved from a peach pit. The dog howling at the moon. All those hours whittling away.

My mother looks through the box of cards people had sent when Granddad died, her Daddy, John Samuel Shannon Baker. All the nice things people said about him. She decides whether to throw them away. I tell her, keep them, keep everything.

The dates are wrong. The records are wrong. The Taggarts are a bit of a mess as well.

I am sending you the new and improved version.

I will go over and over it again to make certain everything is right.

I remember the time she realized the letters he had written from the tuberculosis sanatorium were missing. The x-rays. All of it gone. A child's fear in the doorway, her mother grasping at the empty dresser drawer.

I was looking through another suitcase of Kittie's things. There are so many papers stuffed in odds and ends of notebooks. All of them scribbled with notes. I think she must have driven Samuel wild.

I was the child.

I added the dates the eight children were born. I added the birth for Samuel Shannon. And changed his death. Also that he was Aged 84 yrs. 6 mos. 19 days. I like the way they did that.

I added that Sarah died in her 54th year, which probably means she was 53.

When my mother comes to visit me, it is a week before my 33rd birthday. It is February. My mother takes photographs of the mounds of snow through the window as we drive.

The man at the Historical Society said Samuel Shannon would have been 132 when he died. I hadn't even noticed.

I like the italicized children.

Should I put this back in the folder or in the box? Did I get this out of the file, or was it in the plastic sheet? Now if I put this in here, will we find it again?

I can't remember. There are so many Harriets and Sarahs. I have no idea where Sallie came from, and why is she calling Thomas *Uncle?*

The handwriting is so shaky. I'm sure it was Kittie. If I'd looked at it with my glasses on.

I have all these letters in a book. I need to organize them.

Something has carved a fiery lightning bolt in my mother's eye. I take her to the ophthalmologist, and she says, this is just like when I would visit my mother and we would go to all her doctor's appointments. I stay in the room with her.

Keep everything. Or throw everything away. One or the other. But keep everything.

The ophthalmologist says, Has anyone ever told you you have cataracts? No one has ever told her that before.

I also found a letter Kittie wrote two months before she died. Wasn't signed. It is sort of a rambling letter, how she can just lie on her back. From the pain, I suppose, she doesn't say. She tells a little about her grandmother and how she had 11 children who all lived to maturity. Said she was going to send some flower seeds. And then went into a genealogy rambling about a Thomas Macy who persevered and ended up buying the island of Nantucket. We better go easy or we might end up like this as well.

You are right. Kittie must have made a mistake. In several places.

I'm so exhausted from genealogying. Genealogying is hard work.

I go to the ophthalmologist, and he says my eyes are dry. I go to the dentist, and my teeth and my mouth are dry. It's terrible getting older, my mother says. I'm drying out.

I'm sorry but today I found more papers. There are too many letters to read. Too many people we don't know. I hope I corrected all the Ephraims.

One weekend when I was young, I slept on Fannie's sofa in front of a little fireplace, my mother says. She had the nicest long kitchen. Loved the table and benches she had to eat at. My mind is blank. What is it called? Not open table and chairs but like they have in a restaurant. I hate it when a word goes. Must be my age.

I think I am going to make a nice neat pile of everything I have everywhere and put it in my cupboard.

I'm just going to have a little rest.

She must not have been in the house when the census came through.

* * * * * *

In Those Days
Everyone
Was a
Pillar of the
Community

J.C. Baker's Razor [Private Collection, ca. 1900]

Unhinging like a pocket knife, rusted, I would have thought of
John Columbus' jaw, upper lip, loose hairs tapped from the blade,
little silver commas in a white sink. Funny, I always think of him
as a wild kinked beard. If he wore a bow tie we wouldn't know
about it. I've seen the pictures. Bone handle, bowed to meet the
embrace of a man's thumb, even a heavy man. What did he need
it for? The curve of his neck, knob of his throat. I can almost see
him lifting the heavy veil. A small scratching sound. Here. Hold it
in your hand. Isn't it cold?

Dear Sir, Your father departed this life at ten minutes to four today he died without a groan but suffered great pain last night and for part of today he grew weak very rapidly since Monday night and will be buried on Friday morning at Eleven O'clock I cannot write any more at present.

J.C. Baker is no more. Death came Tuesday and found him calmly waiting.

He was a Christian, the highest style of man.

All thought Thomas Jenkins was dying. The family were called around his bed and he bid them good-bye saying, I'm leaving you now to cross over the river.

Sudden termination of life of one of Mount Carmel's best citizens. Death is a shock. Death has invaded our city. Body expected to arrive tonight.

The clothing was disarranged about the waist, indicating a money belt had been removed but $26 in cash was found in the clothing, which cast some doubt on a robbery theory.

Universal sympathy is freely tendered.

There has been a great deal transpired since last time I wrote to you. We have been called to part with one of the dearest babies. I did not know what it was to lose a friend. It is a month today since we laid him in the ground. Tom will give you the particulars.

Although Miss Jenkins had been blind for the past eight years or more, she was never idle, but always diligently plying her needles and fashioning articles of usefulness and beauty.

She had been suffering for some time and had been very low, but Tuesday she was thought to be better. Tuesday night she grew worse and this morning passed away.

In death Mount Carmel loses one of its noblest Christian women.

How thankful I will always be that I came when I did and I firmly believe that he saved himself to my coming and he was in my arms to the last.

The loved ones were summoned to come with all speed, but while some were still hastening on their way, mother quietly passed on.

Mr. Raum had gone out into the large back yard after dinner to rest. His wife noticed him lying in the shade but thought he was taking a nap. After a while she walked past him and said something. He did not answer. She bent over to touch him.

Know all men by these presents that I being of sound and disposing mind and memory, not laboring under menace, fraud, or undue influence of any person whomsoever, and hereby revoking any and all Wills by me made, so make, publish, and declare this to be my Last Will and Testament. I give to my daughter the sum of Ten Dollars. I give to my son the sum of Ten Dollars.

The doctor reached the house just before he passed away.

We have had a lovely fall until last Friday when it began to rain and today we are having what they call a silver thaw. It is hard to describe, not very cold but ice is frozen all over the trees and wires and it is beautiful but all along it is raining hard which keeps the ice washed off the streets.

Mrs. Shannon answers the death summons at the home she loved so well, 119 West Third Street, this Saturday evening April 18, 6:47pm.

Last night the wind blew hard but today it is quiet as can be.

* * * * * *

To Whom
It May
Concern

Riverview Cemetery, Cynthia Marie Hoffman [July, 2008]

That looks silly. Stand up. Sit back down again. Turn your head so it looks like you're reading her name. Make a serious face. Why are you smiling? Harriet Jenkins, born and died. In remembrance of Sarah. In remembrance of James.

My mother unclasps the gold chain and peels it away from her sunburned neck. It's hurting me, she says.

I'm the one who found the stones, walked right up to them. We went back to Ephraim's grave and found him. No one will forget. We come around full circle.

The woman in the graveyard gives us Cokes. If I hadn't gotten melted chocolate on my white shorts, I'd be a lot cooler right now.

Remembrance Day is when you go to the Riverview Cemetery and you have a white balloon for every person you have buried there. Everyone gathers in a big group and there's some kind of ceremony or something.

This is just a headstone without a head. The bodies are buried beneath the parking lot on the corner of Third and Queen. They only took the stones when they moved.

There is nothing in the file for Jenkins. How do you miss a row of waist-high tombstones? Harriet was born in the 1700s and still you can read all of it. Clearly marked. *Harriet Jenkins.* Who misses that?

Someone reads a poem. And then they release all the balloons into the air all at once. Little white ghosts with shimmery tails.

We get out the shovel. We tear up a bundle of grass. What does it say on this stone? Is it a poem? Get that dandelion out of here.

Who is this Catherine person between Ephraim and his children? Wife of Somebody Something. She's not ours.

My legs are on fire under these jeans.

The card in the file is marked *Van Alen.*

My mother counts up the white balloons. Altogether, we have thirteen.

She ties the balloons together so she can recognize them in the sky. So they don't look like anyone else's. We have found Ephraim, they say. We have found Sarah, James, Ephraim, Ephraim, William, Harriet, Sarah, James, Elizabeth, Elizabeth, Mary Ann. Samuel.

We're sunburned. It hurts to brush our hair.

I'm starting to think no one knows who's buried here. You can't trust anyone. You have to get out and walk the grounds, look at every stone, both sides. I want to tell you, I have a feeling about graves.

You must have inherited it from me.

We could have her moved, the Catherine person. Can't see how it would make a difference seeing as though she doesn't have a body.

The gnats are awful today. Let's get into the air conditioning.

See? Those are the two Elizabeths that were so confusing, the two headstones on the right. They're the ones we said thank goodness they died so we wouldn't have to keep on tracking all those confusing Elizabeths.

Shhh. Stop saying that. They'll hear you.

* * * * * *

Call the cemetery caretaker. Tell her to stop.

Sometimes when my mother calls I think someone has died. Or someone has been reinterred.

To Whom It May Concern:

We had gone after the tombstones with a shovel.

This certifies that I, D.K. Hauck, undertaker, officiated at the removal from the old Presbyterian Burying Ground, Northumberland, Pa., and at the reinterment in the church plot in Riverview Cemetery of the same place, March 5, 1910, the remains of the following named persons:

He has a photograph of the old church. The pastor's house is still standing. He's going to show me where everything was.

We rocked Ephraim's tombstone in the earth to see if we could rock it loose.

Ephraim Patterson Shannon, Sarah wife of E.P. Shannon, Ephraim son of the above named, Ephraim son of the above named, James Jenkins son of the above named.

If they couldn't pay, then only the headstones were moved. Of course the dead weren't around so they couldn't pay.

The tombstones designating the above have also been transferred and properly placed. The Shannons paid, whoever was alive in 1910.

We brushed them with a heavy brush, not a bristle brush, and some plain Wisk.

If the families couldn't pay then the bodies stayed there. The others are still there. In the alley. Under the pavement. He's going to show me where it was. I'll take a picture. This is why we thought we had headstones with no heads.

We come from a family whose bodies are in the ground in the right spot, under the stones. And the stones have the right names on them.

At least there are no bodies, we had said.

And when it is nearly impossible to read the names, my mother has a new stone laid in the ground which will be possible to read forever. And this stone will never chip or fade or wash away or sink into the earth. And if it does, my mother will dig it up again.

See how it says *also*? In addition to the bodies.

To be buried under a tree that will never die, never shrivel from drought or topple over from flood, never to be struck by lightning.

It isn't nice, she says, it's necessary. To be carved into a stone that will never erode.

Of course there is no picture of Sarah. We could always have the bones dug up, have a forensic scientist do a reproduction. Now that we know there are bodies down there.

Sworn and subscribed to before me this seventh day of March, 1910. At least there are no bones, we had said.

Call me when you want to talk about the tombstones.

* * * * * *

Diane
I Think
I Know
What You
Are
Looking For

Single Upright Monument with Oval Top [Monument Engraver's Catalogue, Private Collection, 2008]

One must understand geometry in order to plan a graveyard. Not to think of the dead and their wish to huddle against one another beneath the earth, even in their wooden crates, but first to make allowance for the width of the machine. Hail the gardener who maneuvers among the stones. God bless well-tended flowers, a precisely clipped lawn, calm green waters in which the stones bob in their gray bathing suits. Wish there were room for something poetic. I want to rub chalk on the headstones, so they get it right.

I just don't see why he would have died in Tionesta. His will and deed were in Northumberland.

I went to see the monument man. Asked him what kind of coffins did they use in those days.

Asked if there were a Samuel Shannon in his cemetery. Said no. Said back in those days they didn't keep records, often didn't mark where they buried people.

First, yes, granite is the most durable product used today. It will not weather.

And if Samuel Shannon died in Tionesta, he was probably buried there. Just there where he died. There isn't anything for us to find. There's just nothing.

Shape denotes price, so that is the first decision.

As for the history, I could not have told you it was Samuel Shannon who came from Ireland, only that someone had.

Think about the dimensions to give it that old-time graveyard gravestone look.

Asked why, they could have been burying people on top of each other. Said that was just the way they did it. In those days.

I want to believe they took him home to Northumberland.

None of the Shannon stones have doves. What is this dove thing? The cabinet makers built the coffins. They had the wood.

I want to place a gravestone for Samuel Shannon, in the graveyard, next to his son. I like to think he died there.

I want to create a file on him in both places.

You pay for a plot. You pay for the stone, you pay by the letter, you pay to have it placed.

The first Samuel from Ireland had to run from the authorities because he had been part of a plot to kill the king. First he escaped to France.

In those days, they would put the dead on ice. The only way to notify was by letter.

Such a romantic story stuck in my head.

Also, while I'm doing it, why not a little stone for William?

* * * * * *

Thus
Endeth the
Chapter of
My Life
History

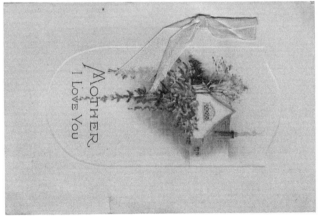

Diane Baker Hoffman, Mending the Mary Wilson Book
[February, 2008. Memory Book ca. 1930, Private Collection]

One hand hovers over the flakes of newspaper like a fortune
teller's hand. In this hand, the tape. In the imaginary third hand,
photographs of our family, my childhood in a jumble, nibbled by
mice in the dark boxes in the dark shelves of the basement. What
is the exact volume of scrap and residue we must leave behind? In
order to be found again. Delicately and with precise hands. Who
will assemble it? I will. I will.

Thus endeth the chapter of my life history to the close of the war.

My mother has her gas line replaced. The earth is turned up like a snake all the way from the street to the house. All day, she smells gas rising up from the basement.

At midnight, the horses stampeded and swept back upon the rear like a whirlwind and in less time than required in the relation of this incident the highway was cleared of every living creature.

The men had forgotten to tighten the crank.

My mother has made a copy of the essay William Henry Hughes wrote about his war experiences in the 1860s at fifteen years of age on behalf of the South. It arrives with a little note: *To Cynthia. Love, William Henry Hughes.*

Do you have your tree?

My father comes in the door. First thing he says, crouching to pet the dog, is I smell gas.

If you go to Mount Carmel you will find a photograph of William Henry Hughes on the Wall of Mayors. If you go with your mother, you can have your photograph taken standing at the wall, with the head of Mayor Hughes between the two of you.

We talk about it later on the phone. My mother says, what if the house had burned down? I told Bill, I said, what about all the genealogy?

Soon after Sherman's evacuation we followed in his tracks over a wasted swath of land which had but a day before blossomed as the rose.

Everyone tells the myth of the Lord Mayor. No one was mayor of Dublin. No one was involved in a plot to kill the king.

Okay. Start with Thomas Jenkins Shannon. Did you find him?
Son of Ephraim and Sarah. Then the children. Look to the right:
Infant, Thomas Shannon (he died), Ephraim Patterson Shannon
(he died), there's Samuel of course, and then Mary. And that's how
we get to William Henry Hughes. Because of Mary.

I've been here enough times. I should remember how to get around.

Look on the list. Where is Samuel Shannon? Whether he ever
lived in Dublin. Whether he escaped to France.

It's just too much trouble to do it all again, my mother had said to
my father. And what are you doing petting the dog?, she said. It's
exhausting. I could have lost everything.

*As a personal history I should note that in one of these skirmishes I
received a scratch bullet wound on the tip of my right shoulder. My
horse, a bullet scratch on the neck.*

* * * * * *

This is an example of what I have been trying to say. Rain in a graveyard is the great equalizer. We add our names to the tree like a death sentence.

Ephraim Patterson Shannon dead James Shannon dead Thomas Jenkins Shannon dead Sarah Jenkins Shannon dead

All the rest, residue, and remainder of my estate I give, devise, and bequeath.

So sad to see the little poems Frances kept to remind her of her mother and father. *A lock of hair from mother's casket*, it says.

I found a few more Bakers on Kittie's side. She was born in Plymouth. Who can help us there?

Isn't that a sad letter? What a sweet man Roy was. I found just one page. It broke my heart.

Mary Frances Shannon dead William Shannon Meriwether Hughes dead William Shannon Hughes dead

If anything should happen to me.

They didn't have a newspaper until the 1860s, did you know that? So there's nothing.

I missed knowing Kittie by three years, my mother says. I missed Roy by three years. If there is no record, we make one. We open a file. Lay down a stone. I pass it on to my daughter.

So sad going through some of these things. Makes me remember the sad times when I lost my parents.

I think I'm pretty much done going through these wads of paper.

Thomas Shannon dead Thomas Shannon infant dead Ephraim Patterson Shannon dead Samuel Shannon dead Samuel Shannon dead Samuel Shannon dead

My favorite people are Ephraim and that woman, what's her name.

Re: Headstones. Re: Samuel Shannon. Sad letter found.

I'll call her and then that's it. She was my last hope.

When your mother is gone, much of you goes with her. This is your childhood, much of which you don't remember.

Kittie Baker Shannon dead Fannie Shannon Baker dead John Samuel Shannon Baker dead Diane Baker living I want her to live forever I want to live forever

This is your Girl Scout sash. This is your badge for charting the growth of trees in the forest.

Pretty certain this is the last of what I will find.

I know who she is.

* * * * * *

Acknowledgments

These poems are for my mother, Diane Baker Hoffman.

With thanks to Dr. Gerald and Lois Ann Burkett for their care-taking of the Shannon house and for their friendship. To Claudia Dant for her research with the Wabash County Museum in Mount Carmel, Illinois. To Carol Crisp for identifying our family graves in Golconda, Illinois. And to Mildred McCormick, posthumously, of the Pope County Historical Society Museum, who gifted us Frances Baker's nightgown.

With gratitude to the fellow poets and friends who read and critiqued this work. To Nick Lantz, Jesse Lee Kercheval, and Katie Ford. With appreciation to Gabriel Fried, Rita Lascaro, and Persea Books.

Grateful acknowledgment is made to the *Texas Review,* in which the first section of this book, "This Is Your Family Tree," first appeared.